EXPLORING
DITCHLING

TEN CIRCULAR WALKS

GW00497935

Janet and Dav

Illustrations
by
John Lord and Denie Trevelyan

S. B. Publications

Introduction

The villages of Ditchling, Streat and Westmeston whose origins go back to Saxon times and beyond are all mentioned in The Domesday Book where Streat has the distinction of having two churches mentioned. In spite of encroaching development throughout the south-east these three neighbouring villages are still bordered to the south by the timeless expanse of the South Downs, to the north by commonland, a means of livelihood for villagers since ancient times, and to the east and west by farmland. The footpaths and bridleways that cross the countryside are the old trackways and drove routes that linked parishes and farms before the turnpike system. Sussex byways are often sunken lanes worn by centuries of boots and hooves and cart wheels. Ditchling, Streat and Westmeston Footpaths Society, which celebrated its 25th anniversary in 1987, works to keep these paths open and to encourage walkers to use and enjoy this heritage. Working parties regularly clear undergrowth or overhanging branches, repair and maintain stiles and erect or replace footpath signs in practical efforts to ensure that the network of paths survives.

The three parishes are unusually long and narrow and all incorporate some downland, the fertile strip below the downs, a small part of the greensand ridge and the heavy wooded clay to the north. The ten walks in this book were chosen as a good representation of the varied countryside which in turn provides habitat for a variety of wildlife. While doing the walks we have been able to watch: hares, barn owl, stoat, sparrowhawk, heron, geese; marbled white, common blue and chalkhill blue butterflies and have seen 8 species of orchid. The footpaths and bridleways of the area offer not only an opportunity to discover its wildlife but also to watch the changing seasons in the countryside. A walk on the Downs on a bright, frosty winter morning is quite another experience from walking there in high summer of waving corn, blue butterflies and bees working among the gorse and herbs. And a Sussex woodland in early spring bursting with birdsong and new green foliage has a very different feel from a golden autumn afternoon six months later!

The ten walks are all circular and start from car parks and have been planned to include as many different paths as possible and to minimise road walking. Five walks set out from The Village Hall Car Park in Ditchling, three from the National Trust Car Park on Ditchling Beacon and two from the East Sussex County Council Car Park on Ditchling Common. The walks are between three and six miles long and are all suitable for family walking, although most of the paths are unsuitable for prams or push-chairs.

It is possible to make some walks longer, for example walk 3 goes from the village through the Beacon Car Park which is the starting point for walks 8, 9 and 10 while Walk 4 from the village passes Ditchling Common, the starting point for walks 6 and 7. For a comprehensive reference to the footpaths of the area we recommend Ordnance Survey Map TQ 21/31 1:25,000. Many of the paths are now waymarked with yellow arrows denoting a footpath and blue arrows denoting bridleway. In this book all maps are drawn with north to the top of the page.

A word of warning — our Sussex paths do tend to become muddy: the bostals up onto the Downs may become very sticky in winter and the woodland and sunken ways of the weald do become very bad at certain times of the year. The state of Sussex roads gave rise to much mockery among travellers in the 18th Century and one of several stories went like this:

> "A traveller in the Sussex countryside came upon a hat lying on top of the mud. When he lifted the hat he found a man beneath it and asked 'Do you require assistance?' Said the man 'Never mind me but look to my horse'. The tale was further exaggerated when the horse was found to be feeding from a cartload of hay lost the previous day!"

It is always advisable to wear stout footwear or wellingtons!

We should also advise walkers that while the details and directions were accurate at the time of going to print, the countryside is vulnerable to change at the hands of farmers, and developers so that pasture may be ploughed, stiles and gates may be changed and footpaths diverted. However, it is the aim of our book to encourage further exploration along footpaths and bridleways thus giving an insight into the three parishes both past and present so that the walker might get to know 'a little bit of his world'.

Walks from Ditchling village

The five walks from Ditchling village set out from the Village Hall Car Park situated 100 yards east of the crossroads. The walks we have chosen follow the four points of the compass, with two heading north, and pass ancient farms, the three parish churches and local landmarks including Ditchling Beacon and Oldland Mill. We do not attempt to describe such points of interest in detail — this will have been done elsewhere — but if you are curious a visit to Ditchling Museum, housed in the old Victorian school north of the church, will prove interesting.

The village of Ditchling has its origins in Saxon times although evidence has been found of occupation in the Stone Age period. The parish church, dedicated to St. Margaret of Antioch dates mainly from the 13th century and you will see all periods of architecture from medieaval to the present represented in the houses as you walk through the village. A general change in working patterns has meant that only a few residents now earn their living by working in the village — most householders travel elsewhere, many commuting to London. A hundred years ago this was not so for Ditchling was a thriving self-contained village where a wide variety of tradesmen served their own community, while the majority of the population were farm labourers and their families. However, modern Ditchling retains a sense of community through its churches, village school and many societies. We hope to show how important the footpaths were to the village and its neighbouring parishes in the past and how enjoyable they can be to the present and future generations.

Walks from the village

Walk 1 *Lodge Hill*

Walk 2 *Three Churches*

Walk 3 *The Beacon*

Walk 4 *Blackbrook Wood*

Walk 5 *Court Garden Farm*

Walk 1 /Lodge Hill/Oldland Mill/ Thatched Inn

A 3 mile circular walk to the west of the village, passing the village pond, Oldland Mill and The Thatched Inn and returning to the village through open fields partly along the Roman Road.

     Park at the Village Hall Car Park. Turn left out of the car park to the crossroads and cross over, keeping in the same westerly direction to pass the timber-framed building, now "Bespoke Stationery" on your left. Pass the White Horse Inn and Wing's Place, a tudor manor house said falsely to be one of those given to Anne of Cleves by Henry VIII. The parish church of St. Margaret is opposite. Continue past 'Cotterlings' with its glazed mathematical tiles, and cross the road passing the War Memorial on your left as you enter Lodge Hill Lane.

     The Village Green on your right, until about 25 years ago, used to be a working farm, Court Farm, and the pond was the watering place for stock; some of the original flint walls of the farmyard remain as do the cart lodge and cow-stalls. The Green is now maintained by The Friends of Ditchling. As you pass the pond on your right you will see the green mound of Lodge Hill rising before you: the hill, said by some to be an ancient burial mound, has now been placed in trust for use by the villagers and every ten years it provides a fitting site for the village pageant.

Follow the lane as it curves left and then climbs with trees on either side that create a leafy tunnel in summer. At the top of the hill you may choose to continue along the lane or, alternatively, to take the footpath that runs through the field on your left parallel to the road.

From the stile on your left you will have fine views and can see three windmills — Jack and Jill on the Downs above Clayton to your left and Oldland Mill to your right. Turn immediately right after climbing the stile and walk with the hedge on your right around the edge of the sloping fields to the stile in the fence and continue to the next stile in the far corner just before Oldland Mill where you rejoin the other route.

For those staying on the lane, walk on past the stile for approx. 300 yards where the lane becomes a rough bridleway and passes gateways to left and right; Court Garden Farm can be seen to the north just before the path runs between bushes to meet the footpath as you approach Oldland Mill.

Walk down the lane with Oldland Mill on your right. The mill is first mentioned in a Ditchling Churchwarden's report dated 1755 and is a post mill. It is now owned by the Sussex Archaeological Society and is in the process of being restored by volunteers from Hassocks Amenity Society and you may like to contribute to this work in the collecting box. Pass Oldland Manor House on your left and you can see Keymer Church across the fields towards the Downs. Keep on this lane for approx. $\frac{1}{4}$ mile until you reach Ockley Lane. Turn left and walk along the wide verge for approx. $\frac{1}{4}$ mile until you see The Thatched Inn on your right: you may like to refresh yourself before setting out across the fields to Ditchling!

Enter the field on your left via the kissing gate and follow the path which runs diagonally to the right across the field and go over the stile to head for the next stile and ditch beside the oak tree at the far side of the field. Cross this stile and ditch and follow the path keeping the fence to your

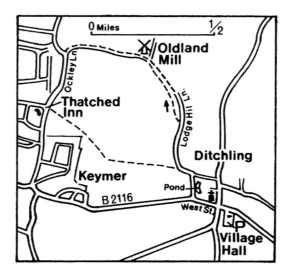

left. The path here is thought to follow the line of the Roman road. You will see ahead of you the distinctive view of Ditchling Church. Follow the path along the edge of the field until you come to the stile beside a gateway taking you into Lodge Hill Lane

Bear right and walk down the lane for approx. 100 yards to Boddingtons Lane ahead of you. Turn up this lane and go through the squeeze gate beside a pair of whitewashed cottages and past allotments on your right to the main road. Turn right down the High Street to the crossroads and then turn left along Lewes Road to the car park 100 yards on the right.

Walk 2 /The Three Churches

A 5 mile circular walk going east out of the village visiting the three parish churches of Ditchling, Streat and Westmeston and returning through open farmland.

27

Park at the Village Hall Car Park. Turn left out of the car park and cross over the crossroads to walk up West Street past the White Horse Inn. By the timber-framed house, Wing's Place cross over the road to the flint church of St. Margaret, built in the 13th century on an elevation. While inside the church you will see the monument to Henry Poole in the Abergavenny Chapel who lived at Wing's Place. After visiting St. Margaret's, follow the path to the north of the church and where it divides take the right hand fork to Church Lane. (The left hand path leads to Ditchling Museum).

Turn right down Church Lane to join the High Street opposite The Sandrock and turn left to walk up the High Street approx. 50 yards and then take the right-hand turning East End Lane. Walk down East End Lane, once the main east-west thoroughfare, for approx. $\frac{1}{4}$ mile until you see a white house, East End House to your right and here take the rough lane, Farm Lane on your left passing what were once farm buildings on the right. Go through the gate into the Recreation Ground but keep to the left of the tennis court and hedge to walk down the wide grass path until you reach a stream and cross via the bridge into a small field to the left of the village cemetery. Make for the far left hand corner of this field and go over the stile onto a narrow footpath which runs above a sandpit disused for 30 years and now a haven for wildlife.

At the end of this path go down the steps and across Spatham Lane to take the farm track opposite to Hayleigh Farm $\frac{3}{4}$ mile away. The farm dates back to the medieaval period and the present farmhouse dates from the 16th century. Pass to the right of farm buildings and, keeping in the same direction, cross the bridleway and go over the stile ahead between fuel tanks. The footpath bears left uphill to the top left-hand corner of the field where you cross another stile and turn right up the rough lane to Streat Church passing the cemetery on your right.

As you enter the churchyard you will see Streat Place, an 'E'-shaped Jacobean house. Two points of interest in the church are the memorial window to Lord Manton, the well-known racehorse breeder who lived at Plumpton Place and the two cast iron memorial slabs set in the floor of the nave. Retrace your steps through the lychgate and right along the rough lane past the telephone box and take the second gate on your left into the cemetery. From here you have a clear view of the line of the Downs and straight ahead is the "V" of trees planted on the hill above Streat to commemorate Queen Victoria's Golden Jubilee.

Go down the brick path and through the kissing-gate to bear right across the field towards the oak tree and cross the stile in the hedge and continue in the same line to approximately the centre of the bottom hedge where you go through another kissing-gate and turn right onto the path running beside a sandpit. The sandpit is still in use and has provided a nesting site for the now declining sandmartin; a remarkable record was made 30 years ago by ornithologists when three pairs of bee-eaters nested in the sandpit! The footpath bears left for a few yards beside the pit and then goes right into a field. Proceed round the edge of the field, keeping the hedge and sandpit on your left, and enter the next field where the path goes diagonally right to a few yards left of the Field Maple tree in the hedgerow approx. 150 yards from the right-hand corner. Go over the stile and turn left up the bridle-lane between hedges.

The path continues straight on and as you walk through the trees you will see Middleton Manor on your left and there is a pond on the right. Continue for $\frac{1}{4}$ mile along the bridleway to an iron gateway across the lane; go through the gate and the path climbs to approach Old Middleton House. Immediately before the stableyard take the narrow footpath on your right and cross the stile into a field turning left to the gateway beside the main road. Cross the road and walk a few yards to the right along the verge entering Westmeston Churchyard opposite via the wooden gate beside a bus shelter.

Enter the parish church of St. Martin through the attractive north porch and one of the notable features inside is the memorial window depicting the Death of Galahad which is in memory of Lieut. Frederick Baines who was killed in Ypres in 1915.

On leaving the church turn right and then left along the path to the north-west corner of the churchyard and the footpath leaves the church down some steps beside a shed out onto the main road. Cross the road and take the footpath to the right in front of flint cottages parallel to the main road and keep on this path past April Cottage until you cross a stile into a field. Continue over the next stile and you will see the medieaval manor house, Westmeston Place to your right. Bear right and climb the next stile beside a garden fence and then bear left across the field passing Pond Farm on your left. Cross a bridge and stile and maintain the same direction through the field to go over the stile near the corner. Cross the next stile a few yards to the right and make for the stile in the opposite hedge again maintaining the same general direction. Go over the stile and the next in the left hand fence and keep on to cross the stile to the right of the garden fence.

Cross the stream and walk along the path between gardens and when you reach the private road, Shirleys, cross over to the telegraph pole and walk along the footpath with a privet hedge on your right. Go through an iron gate and follow the path between hedges out into Lewes Road. Turn left and walk towards the village passing a garage on your left opposite the entrance to East End Lane. Keep walking along Lewes Road and pass the new village school on your right. The village hall car park is approx. 300 yards ahead on the left.

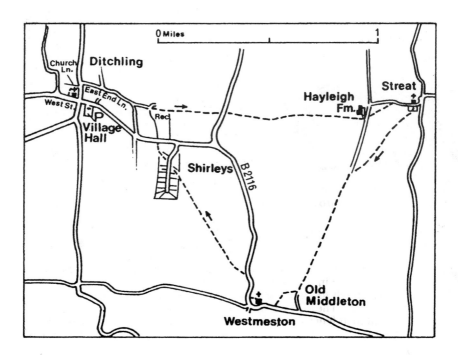

Walk 3 /*The village to Ditchling Beacon*

A 4 mile circular walk heading south from the village to take you past Park Barn Farm and onto the Sussex Trust for Nature Conservation Reserve on Ditchling Beacon, returning past Ditchling Vineyard.

Park at the Village Hall Car Park. Turn left out of the car park and left at the crossroads to walk down South Street passing the Jointure on your right which was the home of the artist Frank Brangwyn. Where the road forks and South Street joins Beacon Road, cross over to the white signpost and take the footpath which runs between fences until it reaches a housing estate. The footpath sign on the lamp-post points you between houses beside a sign reading Nevill Flats 21-24. Go along this path and over the bridge and stile into a field.

Turn left towards the Downs and walk behind gardens to cross a stile in the hedge. The path now narrows, running between the hedge on your left and field fence on your right. Turn left at the oak tree where the houses end and go over the bridge turning right through the next field with the Downs before you. Pass a gate and stile beside the road and then go through the next field keeping in the same direction with the fence and stream on your right. Climb the stile into a copse which you cross before entering a paddock via another stile.

Now head for the farm buildings and the path goes between the pole barn and asbestos farm building and through a gate. Cross the farm lane and walk to the left of the loose boxes and turn right on entering the wood. Follow the path through the wood and you will see Park Barn farmhouse to your left; go over the stile and into a field. Keep straight on towards the Downs to the stile in the right corner of the field which takes you into Underhill Lane. Turn left along Underhill Lane to the crossroads.

*A shorter route, avoiding the steep ascent to Ditchling Beacon takes you straight over the crossroads and follows the lane for approximately $\frac{1}{4}$ mile until you come to Nye Lane bridleway on your left. You rejoin the main walk at the asterisk below.

Turn right at the crossroads and take the footpath ahead of you which runs to the left of the fieldgate. Go over the stile and up the steep path from which you have a good view across the fields to your right of Wolstonbury Hill. The path climbs through bushes up the side of the Downs and immediately after the next stile take the left fork up a chalky slope. Pause on the knoll for the first of many fine views of the village of Ditchling. Continue up the path with a chalk quarry on your left.

This part of the Downs is managed by the Sussex Trust for Nature Conservation to encourage the growth of such typical Downland species as twayblade, scabious, round-headed rampion and orchids thus maintaining the chalk grassland character. The path levels out before going down a steep bank and turns right at the bottom to curve through ash trees and on to the top of the Downs. This part of the path is known locally as The Slype and thought to be a pre-Roman trackway.

As you approach the ridge the path leads into an open field and bears left parallel with the escarpment. Walk east along the path which climbs slightly to reach Ditchling Beacon, one of the highest points on the South Downs at 813 feet above sea level, and the site of an early iron-age settlement. Keep along the trackway which leads to the National Trust Car Park. You can see to the south-east Mount Caburn, Firle Beacon, the beginning of the Seven Sisters and Seaford Head.

Go straight through the car park to the road and turn left keeping to the grass verge and where it ends cross the road onto the opposite verge following the fence-line; Westmeston Church and Farm can be seen below to your right. Soon the bridleway drops below the road level still following the fence-line on your right.

The steep chalk grassland turf of the Downs is frequented by rabbits although their numbers fluctuate due to outbreaks of myxomatosis; this is hunting ground for the sparrowhawk and kestrel and the summer territory of blackcap, linnet and willow warbler. Several species of orchid occur in this area and you pass the wayfaring tree, characteristic of the Downs.

Where the fenceline ends the path carries on down with ash trees on the right and then bends through trees and bushes. Keep on the bridlepath as it descends to reach Underhill Lane. Turn left along the lane for approx. 100 yards and turn right down Nye Lane Bridleway. *The short walk rejoins here. Proceed down the path with a large hollow on your left and Ditchling Vineyard on your right. The path becomes a concrete drive and where it turns left you keep straight on with woodland on your left.

The path enters the trees and you keep straight on ignoring paths to right and left and where you meet with a hollow-way, walk above and to the left of it until you come to a gate and stile. Go over the stile and straight down the field with hedge and hollow trackway on your right and cross the next stile then bear diagonally left and over the stile in the corner of the field. Proceed in the same direction to cross the stile beside the oak tree in the hedge and walk diagonally across the paddock to climb the stile beside the water trough. Walk up the lane between hedges and straight up the driveway to the main road. Turn left at the road and walk 50 yards to the Village Hall Car Park.

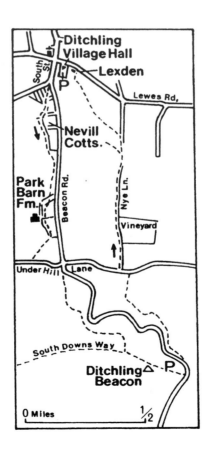

Walk 4 /*Ditchling Village/Blackbrook Wood/Kents Lane*

A 6 mile circular walk to the north and west of the village taking you to the southern end of Ditchling Common via the old droveway returning through woods and open farmland.

   Park at the Village Hall Car Park. Turn right out of the car park for a few yards and cross the road to The Twitten. Walk up the Twitten (the name is peculiar to this region meaning 'betwixt and between') and pass the Unitarian Church on your left which was built c. 1740. The Twitten slopes down to East End Lane, cross the lane and go straight on up The Dymocks and where this lane bears left uphill go straight on taking the footpath between hedge and laurels and over stiles into a field. After a few yards climb another stile in the hedge on your left and turn immediately right so that the same hedge is now on your right, making for the stile ahead in the corner of the field. The path now goes diagonally through the field crossing the stile and ditch in the right-hand hedge about 30 yards from the corner; you are heading in the direction of the farm buildings. Turn immediately left and cross the farm track passing farm buildings on your right and walk straight on down the grassy path. Go over the stile and ditch to the right of the gateway and continue up the field beside the hedge on your left.

   Immediately before the stile and gateway the path turns right becoming a wooded track which is the old droveway from Ditchling Common to the village. Keep on this path crossing a stile and when you reach gateways to right and left the path swings left staying among the trees. This place is known locally as 'Fairy Glen' and is particularly pretty in the Spring when there are clumps of primroses beside the path. Keep on the path until you reach a stile between two trees to the left of a gateway which takes you into a small field.

Walk along the edge of the field keeping the hedge on your right to the next gateway recessed in the right-hand corner. Climb over the gate and walk ahead with the hedge now on your left to the stile in the hedge ahead crossing into the next field and keep in the same direction with the hedge on your left although the path now veers slightly to the right. Go through the gap in the hedge and on over the next stile in the hedge in front of you between the corner and the oak tree. Continue straight on over the next stile and then through the narrow field to the stile in the opposite left-hand corner which takes you back among the trees onto the old drove route.

Pass stiles either side of the path and after the tiled barn on your right go over the stile across the path and walk on through trees to a clearing with a gate on your left and climb the stile ahead of you and after a short distance another stile takes you onto Ditchling Common. Head across the field keeping just to the left of the telegraph pole and pass to the left of a group of bushes ahead of you. Go through the gate onto the railway bridge and cross the bridge, turning right after the next gate to walk towards a cottage with the railway on your right. At the corner turn left passing the gateway and tile-hung cottage and walk beside the hedge following the fenceline to cross the stile in the far corner beside a cottage driveway. Turn right down the driveway for a few yards and go through the iron stile and across the field keeping the trees on your left. Climb the stile in the bottom corner and walk along the path between the fence and oak trees crossing the stile beside a gate into Spatham Lane.

Cross the lane to the right of the signpost and walk for approx. 100 yards up the road passing a bridleway sign on your left, until you reach the gateway into Blackbrook Wood on your right. You will see three paths in front of you, take the middle path through the wood directly ahead of you. This part of the wood is predominantly coppiced hazel with some hornbeam and silver birch with willow and standing oak; in Springtime parts of the wood are carpeted with bluebells. Pass a tall fir tree (Spruce) on your right and a little farther along is an even larger tree and just after this is a crossway of paths; go straight over and the path widens where it meets another path and you bear left along the track keeping to this path through the wood. Go straight over the next crossway turning neither right nor left. Walk past a gate on your right and then, after a few more yards, you pass gates to right and left; to the left you can see the thatched roof of Gallops House.

Take the main path which bears left and runs parallel to a field for approx. $\frac{1}{4}$ mile — this part of the wood is known as The Plantation — and where it reaches the end of the wood you will see a stile ahead. Do not cross the stile but turn right a few yards before you reach it. The wide ride may become muddy in winter and it is advisable to walk among the trees either side where necessary. This old bridleway is called Kents Lane and takes you out of the wood to run alongside a field fence on your right and hedge on the left. From here you have a good view of the Downs in front of you and can see Jack and Jill windmills in the west. Continue down the path and across the farm track to go under the railway arch.

Bear slightly left using the wooden bridge to cross the stream passing to the left of Meadowsweet Cottage to go through the bridlegate into a field. Keep left through the field and next bridlegate and straight on up the track passing a stile on your right and gateways either side. Continue between hedges and, approx. 50 yards before the cottage, turn right over a stile taking the path to the left-hand corner of the field. Cross the bridge into the next field and turn right down the edge of the field for about 50 yards to

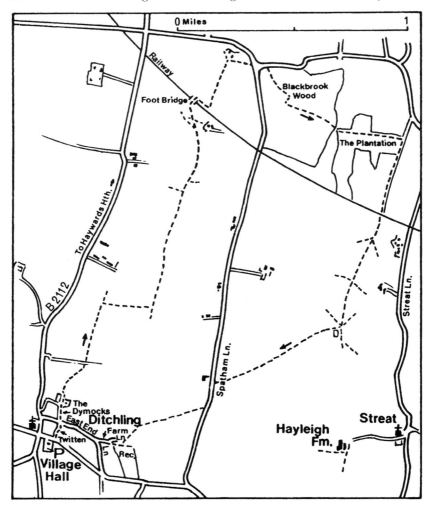

the two oaks on your right where the path now goes diagonally left through the centre of the field. Go over the stile and ditch and continue in the same direction, cutting the corner of the field to cross two ditches and go through the gap in the hedge when the path follows the same line through the field to the trees opposite.

After crossing the stream via a bridge, go up the steps and over the stile where the path bears left across the next field to the stile half-way along the opposite hedge. Spatham Farm can be seen on your right. Go over the stile and walk through the field keeping to the left of the oak tree and cross the next stile and immediately over another stile to your left. Keep in the same direction you have been following over the last two fields to the stile in the hedge across this narrow field and out into Spatham Lane. Turn left along the lane for approx. 300 yards and just past the entrance to the sewage works on your right climb the stile beside a gateway and cross the field diagonally to the far left-hand corner and cross a stile beside a stream into the north field of Ditchling Recreation Ground which is used as a rugby pitch.

Go diagonally left across this field (if no game is in progress!) to the far corner. Now turn right between hedge and garden hedges with the Rec. on your left. Pass the swings and tennis court on your left and go through the gate and along the rough lane, Farm Lane.

Cross the road and take the footpath between two white houses, Pardons and East End House, to a kissing-gate. Go through the gate and continue straight on with bungalows on your left passing a 'Gazebo' which is in the garden of Pardons on your right. Go through the next kissing-gate and along the private road Fieldway. Turn right at the main road to the car park 100 yards on your left.

Walk 5 /Court Garden Farm/Wellhouse Lane/Ditchling Common

A 4 mile circular walk to the north-west of the village passing the ancient Court Garden Farm, crossing the southern edge of Ditchling Common via Wellhouse Lane and returning through fields.

Park at the Village Hall Car Park. Turn left out of the car park and right at the crossroads to walk up the High Street passing The Bull and The Sandrock on your right. At the top of the High Street you pass East End Lane and approx. 50 yards further on take the rough lane East Gardens on your right. Walk approx. 150 yards up this lane and where it bears right take the footpath signed 'To North End' beside the driveway to Grove House. The path runs between a hedge and fence to the left of the white farmhouse, and soon passes allotments on the left and finally coming out onto an estate of retirement homes known as Dumbrell's Court built on land formerly part of Dumbrell's School. Walk along the tarmac path with fence on your left and where the houses end carry on down the roadway to the main road. You pass buildings which used to be part of North End Farm and are now the Turner–Dumbrell Workshops.

At the main road turn right and walk northwards for approx. 200 yards, cross the road and take the farm track passing the entrance to Orchard Lane and climb the stile on your left beside a pine tree. Turn right to walk along the edge of the field with hedge and farm track on your right, heading towards Court Garden Farm. The farm was mentioned in deeds soon after Domesday as the Manor of the Garden and was given to the monks at Lewes by William de Warenne. Pass the farmhouse on your right keeping to the field and go through the field gateway to your right and then through the gateway on your left, passing to the left of farm buildings. Walk beside the fence passing a clump of pine and oak trees on your right and half way along the fence go through the gateway into the adjoining field. Now turn left to walk alongside the fence to the corner of the field and climb the stile to drop down into the hollow way.

Turn right and keep to this bridleway for approx. $\frac{1}{4}$ mile and you will see a black and white timbered farmhouse across the field to your left. Pass the buildings of Broadhill Farm on your left and proceed up the farm lane to Ockley Lane. Turn right along Ockley Lane for approx. $\frac{1}{4}$ mile and then take Wellhouse Lane to your right. Walk up this lane which has attractive views of the Downs across the fields on your right and towards the end of the lane you pass Well House before the entrance to Wellhouse Farm where the footpath goes into a field via a stile opposite the farm. Turn left to walk down the field and go over the stile in the left-hand corner beside an ornamental pond and through the next field, keeping the hedge to your left.

Pass a clump of oak trees on your left and continue through the gateway ahead keeping in the same easterly direction with field on your right and a thick hedge and trees on the left. Pass into the next field with a small pond on your right and single oak tree to the left. You will soon be approaching the main road and might pause a moment here to appreciate the views as the Downs stretch from east to west. Go over the next stile and up the short track to the main road. Cross the road and turn left for about 50 yards to the stile beside a gateway on your right which takes you onto Ditchling Common.

The official bridleway goes towards the centre of the field to the right of the trough and at the time of writing the path passes through two posts which once marked the bridlegate. Continue to the brow of the hill approx. 100 yards before the railway bridge; now turn at right angles to your right to descend towards the far corner (where you in fact meet the far end of the hedge which was to your right on entering the field). Go over the stile onto the old drove track between the Common and Ditchling village and over the next stile crossing a clearing beside a gateway and through the bushes ahead. This is an attractive leafy path but can be difficult, getting muddy in winter and inclined to be overgrown in summer! Cross the next stile and 100 yards past the tiled barn (now collapsed!) on your left are stiles either side of the path, take the stile on your right into a field.

Turn immediately left and walk with the hedge on your left over a sleeper bridge and bear right round the edge of the field and with the hedge still to your left walk to the corner near the nursery. Cross the stile and bridge and walk through the next field passing to the left of the greenhouses and over the next stile and ditch continuing in the same direction beside the hedge on your left to cross the next stile. Walk straight ahead through the gap in the hedge and continue in a southerly direction through the narrow field enjoying the views before you as you walk. Go over the next stile and ditch maintaining the same line and cross the next stile and field where the western end has been planted as a vineyard. Climb the stile to the right of the mound and cross the field which at the time of writing is used for grazing sheep and geese while being considered as the subject of a planning application. The buildings at the western end are known locally as the 'Cottage Homes' and are retirement homes for the Thames Watermen. Go over the stile in the hedge on your left beside a small pond and turn right to cross the stile a few yards ahead.

Walk past the house with two ornamental ponds and the footpath bears round the fenceline and over the ditch and stile in the corner. The

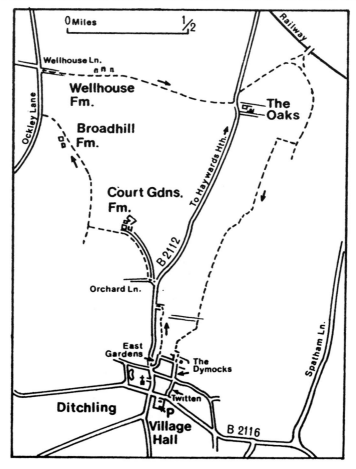

path now heads slightly left making for the middle of the three oak trees in front of you. Go over the stile beside the gap and down the next field keeping the hedge to your right and cross the stile beside a gateway. Keep on the grassy track with hedge and ditch to your right and pass the farm buildings on your left. Cross the farm track and walk along the path still with hedge and ditch on your right for about 20 yards. Climb the stile to your right and walk diagonally towards the far left-hand corner of the field to cross the stile beside a gateway and walk beside the hedge on your left and cross the stile in the corner. Turn immediately right walking 20 yards beside the same hedge and then cross the stile walking between the house and laurel hedge to Dymocks Lane. Continue straight ahead along The Dymocks to East End Lane and cross over to walk up the Twitten past the Unitarian Church, to Lewes Road and the car park opposite.

Walks from Ditchling Common

The two walks from Ditchling Common start from the East Sussex County Council Car Park east of the Common crossroads. Ditchling Common is now managed as a Country Park by the County Council to ensure that the activities of visitors, walkers and horse-riders are compatible with the conservation of commonland. The common was part of the Manor of Ditchling, overseen by the Reeve, and villagers holding commoners' rights could graze cattle, horses and sheep although the grazing of geese was forbidden! A feast was held annually at the Royal Oak, to the north of the common, known as Horn Fair when cattle were brought to be left in the charge of the Reeve for the summer months. In autumn commoners might cut bracken for bedding. More recently, the common has been used for recreation: a summer holiday haunt for boys with bicycles and fishing-rods, for blackberry gathering and picnics or just for walking along the many paths, through high bracken in summer or beside a bluebell haze in springtime.

Walks from The Common

Walk 6 *St. George's Retreat*

Walk 7 *St. Helena Farm*

Walk 6 /Ditchling Common/St. George's Retreat

A 3 mile circular walk to the north of Ditchling Common through woods and returning through the grounds of St. George's Retreat passing close to The Royal Oak.

Park at Ditchling Common Car Park. Start from the middle of the three parking areas and, with your back to the road, walk north over the grass bank ignoring the bridle-track to your immediate right to walk up the next right-hand path about 20 yards on. Go through the staggered rails, cross another bridlepath and continue ahead winding through the bushes and ignoring paths to right and left. Walk past a cottage hedge on your right and cross over the drive to the Industrial Complex then follow the path ahead until you reach a tile-hung cottage. Although the path appears to carry on, the public footpath turns to the right then immediately left to proceed between fences to a rough road. Turn left past cottages along the road until it becomes a grassy path, muddy in winter. Cross the wooden bridge and where the way divides take the left-hand path, walking with the field to your left.

Continue along the wooded path and you come to West Wood, an area of neglected coppice woodland planted with hornbeam which was generally used for firewood but being a hard wood was also used for the heads of mallets. Go over the ditch and, keeping the fence on your left, cross another ditch where you may glimpse the buildings of St. George's Retreat across the fields to your left. The fence represents the boundary between the parishes of Ditchling and Westmeston and you are walking on the Westmeston side. Pass a group of mature conifers on your left and the path now begins to go downhill as it leaves the wood.

When you reach the tile-hung cottage on your right, turn left over the stile beside a gate and walk along the edge of the field keeping the hedge to your right. Cross the next stile beside a gateway and continue in the same direction to climb the next stile and the path turns left passing to the right of a line of oak trees.

*If, however, you feel thirsty or hungry and the time is right, you may wish to carry straight on after the stile for a few more yards and you will find a stile in the hedge to your right which leads you to the main road across the Common opposite The Royal Oak.

The walk continues between an orchard and chicken houses to the right and woodland known as Purchase Wood to the left. St. George's Retreat, to your right, was built in the latter half of the 19th Century as a Catholic Mental Hospital and is today still run by nuns who care for the elderly. The Retreat stands in a park-like setting where the lake attracts large numbers of Canada Geese and provides a fishing ground for heron.

Go over the stile and across the driveway to climb the next stile heading for the bottom left-hand corner of the field. Go through the gate beside the lake and up the farm track, passing to the right of the barn. The footpath now bends slightly to the right and up through the next field. Go over the stile in the hedge and cross the field passing a house on your right and the Industrial Complex on the left to cross another stile in the fence. Walk over the drive to a stile and drop down a steep bank, turning left along the hollow way and then right and sharp right again through the gorse onto Ditchling Common. Walk down the path and across the bridle-track, going through the staggered rails and follow the path down to the car park on your left.

24

Walk 7 /Ditchling Common/St. Helena Farm/Blackbrook Wood

A 4½ mile circular walk to the west of Ditchling Common passing Middleton Common and St. Helena Farms returning through fields and woodland.

Park in Ditchling Common Car Park. Start from the middle of the three parking areas and, with your back to the road, walk north over the grass bank ignoring the bridle-track to your immediate right to walk up the next right-hand path about 20 yards on. A short way on go through the staggered rails, cross another bridlepath and continue ahead winding through the bushes and ignoring paths to right and left. Walk past a cottage hedge on your right and cross over the drive to the Industrial complex then follow the path ahead until you reach a tile-hung cottage. Although the path appears to carry on, the public footpath turns to the right and immediately left to proceed between fences to a rough road, Dobels Lane. Turn left along the lane past cottages until the way becomes a grassy path, often muddy in winter. Now you will see a gate on your right where the old footpath used to go — it has now been diverted 100 yards ahead continuing on over the wooden bridge and then turning sharp right through bushes and over a stile beside a gate into the field.

Walk across the field keeping the hedge and two mature oak trees to your left and cross the stile just after the second oak. Walk east with the hedge on your right to climb the stile in the corner, continuing in the same direction still keeping the hedge on your right. You will come to Middleton Common Farm on your right where the Guernsey herd provides delicious cream from the Farm Shop which deserves a visit too for the range of home-made pies, cakes and bread! When you reach the next stile do not climb over but turn left and walk alongside the hedge for approx. 60 yards to the stile on your right passing the electricity pole, and cross into the next field. Walk east keeping oak, ash and cherry trees on your left. Pass the house and garden and go over the stile in the corner of the field to cross One Hundred Acre Lane.

Go over the stile into a field where the path bears slightly left keeping parallel with and just to the right of the overhead electricity line. The next stile, in the far left-hand corner leads into a garden which you cross keeping the house on your right and going under the weeping willow to cross the stile in the fence into a field where the aspect is spoilt by the eyesore of modern agriculture on your left!

Bear right and make for the right hand corner of the field to go over a stile between hornbeam and ash trees. This field, formerly Hunts Wood has recently been cleared. The path goes straight ahead and over a stile in the fence continuing in the same direction towards the farm you can see three fields distant. Climb the next stile and walk through the field passing a solitary oak on your left to cross the small stream by a bridge and then on up a bank to cross the stile beside an oak tree. As you approach St. Helena Farm go over the ditch via a sleeper bridge and stiles and the footpath passes to the north of the farm so that the farm buildings are on your right. Continue in the same direction over the next stile ignoring the stile on your right. Walk straight along the edge of the field with the fence on your left and climb the stile in the far corner by the oak tree to the left of the bungalow. Cross the garden going under the chestnut tree keeping the bungalow on your right; go past the fish pond and down the drive which leads into the road.

Through the gateway opposite you have extensive views of the downs including Malling Down above Lewes to the east. Turn right down the road to the bend, approx. 150 yards, then turn left down the drive past Inholmes Cottage on your left. Pass a modern bungalow and join a tree-lined green lane which may become muddy in winter when it is advisable to walk above the path among the trees on your left. Keep on this bridleway which narrows into a wooded path with fields on either side. Carry on along the path and you will see Dean Farm across the fields; now bear right over a wooden bridge and follow the path through trees to bear left through a gate into the field. Turn immediately right and walk up the field beside a hedge with the farm across the field to your left. Go through the gate into the farm lane and turn right up the lane; just before you reach the drive leading to Briggs Farm turn right between bushes and a fence to go over a stile in the hedge ahead. The footpath follows a direct line through the field to the gate in the opposite corner taking you into Streat Lane; Glebe Farm Cottage is across the road.

Cross the road and, swinging to the right, go over a stile beside a gate and through the field bearing slightly right towards the opposite hedge and cross a stile into the woods. This part of the wood is known as The Plantation comprising oak, ash and hazel; in springtime there is wealth of bluebells as well as the song of the chiffchaff whose loud call dominates the woodland at this time of the year. A little farther along you come to a grove of horse-chestnuts which, unusually, have been coppiced as it is more often the sweet chestnut which is planted for coppicing. The path through The Plantation is approx. $\frac{1}{4}$ mile long and at the end you will come to gateways to left and right. Through the gateway on your right can be seen the thatched roof of Gallops House and to the left Ditchling Beacon rises away across the fields. A short distance on you pass another gateway on the left; proceed on into Blackbrook Wood of neglected coppice hornbeam, standing oak and some silver birch.

When you come to the first crossway of paths carry on straight over and down a gentle slope to take the right-hand fork. Stay on this path which passes a fir tree (Spruce) and you are now walking among neglected hazel coppice probably last coppiced between the wars. Pass another large fir tree on your left and continue along the path until you reach a gateway leading out onto the road. Turn left along the road passing the junction with Spatham Lane on your left and walk approx. $\frac{1}{4}$ mile along the road back to the car park passing Ditchling Common Industrial Complex on your right which is built on the site of the old Ditchling Brickworks and Potteries.

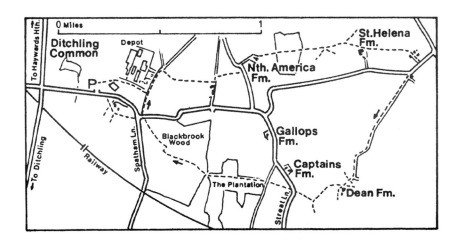

Walks on the Downs

The three downland walks all start from the National Trust Car Park on Ditchling Beacon.

The South Downs, designated as an area of Outstanding Natural Beauty by The Countryside Commission, stretch from Eastbourne in the east into Hampshire in the west, creating a natural division of great beauty between the south coast and the Sussex Weald. The walks head south over open downland which, in times past, would have been predominantly sheep grazed although some land was under the plough being cultivated by teams of oxen. Sheep grazing helped to maintain the typical downland turf with its rich variety of summer herbs and flowers but now many of the sheep are gone and the solitary shepherd is a figure of the past. While much of the Downs is now arable some areas, including Ditchling Beacon, are managed as reserves by the Sussex Trust for Nature Conservation or The Nature Conservancy Council whose aims are to preserve the downland flora and fauna in its chalk grassland habitat. There is still a wealth of wildlife to be seen there including orchids, breeding birds and butterflies; and still the marvellous views and the moments of tranquillity which over the centuries have endeared The South Downs to such writers as Gilbert White, W.H. Hudson and Richard Jefferies.

Walks on The Downs

Walk 8 *St. Mary's Farm*

Walk 9 *High Park Wood*

Walk 10 *Standean Farm*

Walk 8 /Ditchling Beacon/St. Mary's Farm/Streathill Farm

A 4½ mile circular walk heading south from the South Downs Way to St. Mary's Farm in the valley bottom, climbing back to the ridge passing close to Plumpton Plain and back along the South Downs Way.

Park at Ditchling Beacon Car Park. Leaving the car park cross the road and go over the stile beside a bridlegate. Walk eastwards along the track which is part of the South Downs Way, the long distance path across the Downs marked by the Acorn Waymarker. Keep to this track with the fence to your right for approx. ¼ mile until you reach a bushy area on the right and where the bushes end turn right and go through the bridlegate into the field.

Follow the path through this field for approx. ½ mile and then go through the gate and continue down the path. As you walk through this long field you may be accompanied by the song of the skylark soaring high above you, a familiar sound on the Downs. The path leads down into a hollow and curves up the other side with a bank of scrub on the left; this area of bushy cover provides nesting sites for summer visitors such as blackcap, whitethroat and linnet. In spring and summer violets and orchids grow on the bank.

Go through a bridlegate and the path now runs above a valley to your right. Pass a tiger-trap and bridlegate in the fence on the right and keep to the main path; as it begins to descend you may glimpse the buildings of Sussex University among the trees ahead of you. The valley to your left is known as Shambledean Bottom. The track drops down to St. Mary's Farm comprising a group of cottages and farm buildings. Go through the gateway and the farm lane leads to Falmer village but our way turns left passing to the left of the cottages and through the gate. Bear left up the flint track with a wooded area on your right. The clumps of gorse, or 'furze' beside the track exude their distinctive 'almond' scent for much of the year recalling the saying "When furze is out of bloom love is out of tune"!

After about half a mile you reach open fields on your right and then a wooded area to the left. If you turn here and look back you can see Brighton Racecourse and the sea beyond and to your left Castle Hill and Kingston Down. Keep along the track and when you reach the group of trees on your right look across the valley to Plumpton Plain where the bushy area marks the site of a Bronze Age Settlement. The nature writer W.H. Hudson, writing at the turn of the century, mentions this area as one of sheep and furze but now it is largely under the plough.

Pass Streat Hill Farm on your left and continue to the end of the track where you will have extensive views of the Weald to the north. Go through the gate which takes you back onto the South Downs Way and turn left to cross the farm lane and go through another gate. Walk along the South Downs Way across this fairly open stretch of downland for about one mile back to the Car Park.

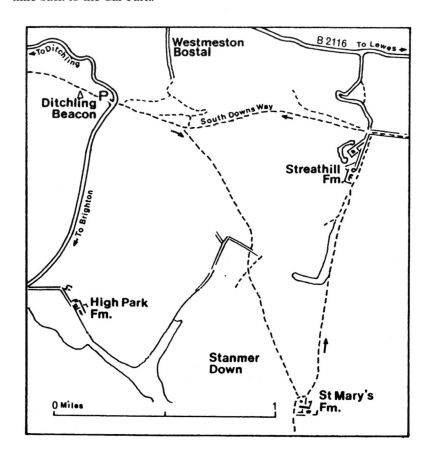

Walk 9 /Ditchling Beacon/Moon's Bottom/ High Park Wood

A 4 mile circular walk heading south-east from Ditchling Beacon into Moon's Bottom, through High Park Wood and returning over downland. The walk goes to within half a mile of the picturesque village of Stanmer.

Park at Ditchling Beacon Car Park. Leaving the car park, cross the road and go over the stile beside a bridlegate. Walk in an easterly direction along the track, which is part of the long distance path, the South Downs Way, until you reach a bushy area on your right and where the bushes end, go through the bridlegate into the field. Follow the track down through the field for approx. $\frac{1}{2}$ mile and go through the gate, continuing down the grassy path into a hollow and up the other side where the path is bordered by bushes and scrub. In spring and summer violets and orchids grow on the bank to the left and the bushy cover provides nesting sites for blackcap, whitethroat and yellowhammer. The path runs up to go through a bridlegate and after a few yards turn right through another bridlegate and down the track into the valley known as Moon's Bottom.

The grassy slope on the left is too steep for cultivation and demonstrates the difference in sward as lack of ploughing has encouraged the growth of downland flowers and herbs which provide food plants for butterflies such as Common Blue and Chalkhill Blue. The clumps of beech trees are probably remnants of Stanmer Park which lies to the south and would have been planted for landscape but also providing cover for game.

The path winds through the valley going through a bridlegate into the next field. Walk straight on, keeping to the edge of the field with trees on your right and after approx. 300 yards enter the wood through the next bridlegate. As you walk up the track it is pleasing to see dead wood left at the side of the path among the trees for this dead and decaying wood provides habitat for insects and is the first stage in the woodland eco-system. In springtime the woodland floor is covered in dog's mercury, a first sign of spring, as well as violets, ragged robin, red campion and wood anenomes.

At the top of the path, beside the electricity pylon you reach a crossway of paths: the path straight in front of you will take you down to Stanmer village about half a mile away and you may like to take time to visit this small, unspoilt village with its working farm, pond, and pretty Victorian church beside Stanmer House in its parkland setting. The path to your left leads to the Sussex University campus and our walk turns right in a northerly direction under the power lines.

Keep to this track all the way through High Park Wood where you will pass some fine beech trees. Over the flint wall on your right are attractive downland views. After approx. $\frac{1}{2}$ mile you pass the buildings of High Park Farm on your right when the track swings to the left; through the trees in spring you will see the blue haze of bluebells carpeting the

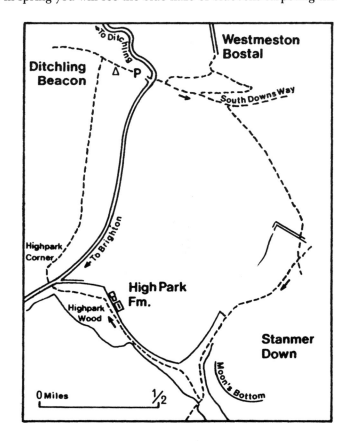

woodland floor. After approx. ¼ mile you pass a corrugated barn on your right and after a few more yards turn sharp right towards the road. Cross the road and go through the bridlegate straight opposite and follow the path down the fenceline on your left to another gate. Go through this gate and turn right following the fenceline along the top of the field to go through the gateway in the far corner. Follow the track between fences and go through the next gateway across the track ignoring the bridlegate on your right; this track is used by cattle and so is liable to become muddy in winter.

You are now walking north back towards the ridge of the Downs and the Beacon Car Park. Keep straight on through an open field with the fence to your right and the valley to your left which is known as Hogtrough Bottom. Go through the next gate and on up the track which brings you onto the South Downs Way. Turn right along the SDW until you reach the car park.

Walk 10 /Ditchling Beacon/ Standean Farm

A 4½ mile circular walk heading south from Ditchling Beacon along downland tracks and through valley bottoms to Lower Standean Farm returning along the South Downs Way with many fine views along the way.

Park at Ditchling Beacon Car Park. Take the South Downs Way track which leads up shallow steps away from the car park for approx. 150 yards and then take the path that rises to your left before the Sussex Trust for Nature Conservation sign. After a short distance turn to your left at the waymarker and the path heads south running parallel to the fence on your right. The path is edged with typical downland scrub of gorse and hawthorn and in the summer there is an abundance of willowherb. You come through the scrub area and into a field keeping in the same direction and now walking parallel with the road over the Downs to Brighton. Look to the left for views of Firle Beacon, Mount Caburn and Seaford Head, and to the south you see the English Channel stretching beyond the town of Brighton.

Keep on the path until you reach a flint track where the way turns right at right-angles. The track takes you approx. 200 yards through the field to a gateway, turn left through the bridlegate and walk down the track with fences on either side. You may well see downland species such as meadow-pipit, cornbunting and skylark alighting on the fenceposts for long enough to be identified!

The path leads through a gateway ahead and straight on down into the valley. Walk through the valley to the bridlegate and continue through the middle of the next field with a fence to your right and scrub-covered slope to the left, passing a solitary sycamore tree on the right. This stretch of open downland with permanent pasture on the steeper banks is an area for hare and partridge and you might be lucky enough to see a group of hares and watch their apparently 'mad' antics from a distance.

The path heads through the gateway in the far corner and then turns left to follow the track curving through the valley then bears right up the hill and on through another gateway. The flint track descends with the buildings of Lower Standean Farm below to the left. Turn right at the old ash tree and follow the farm track which rises gently passing a brick and flint farm building on the left. Go through a gap in the hedge and bear sharp left walking uphill round the edge of the field and then swing to the right still keeping the hedge on your left.

When you reach the gateway to your left at the crossway of bridlepaths, turn right heading in a northerly direction through the middle of the field. Go through the gateway into the next field and follow the track towards the ridge of the Downs where you will meet the South Downs Way. As you walk up this bridlepath, look to your left where you will see the village of Pyecombe with its Norman Church nestling above the busy A23; the hills rising in the west are Wolstonbury Hill, Newtimber Hill and the Devil's Dyke. The famous Jack and Jill windmills can also be seen on your left; Jill, which has now been restored to working order, is used to grind corn and is open to the public on Sundays from Easter until October. When you reach the ridge it is worth pausing for a while to take in the superb views in all directions.

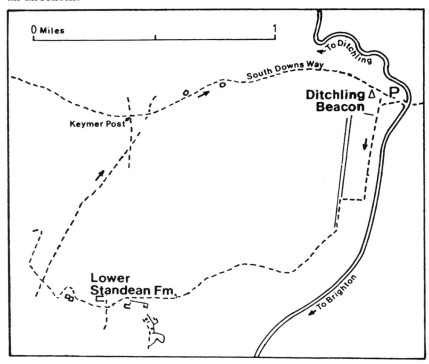

Turn right along the South Downs Way through the gate which bears the SDW Acorn Waymarker. Walk straight ahead along the track, with the Weald stretching below to your left, and on through the next gate to pass a dewpond on your left. The dewponds on the Downs are large bowl-shaped depressions dug for the watering of grazing stock, mainly sheep; they were dug out and lined with clay and straw to retain water. The extensive cover of gorse here provides valuable nesting habitat for downland birds.

Keep on the path, passing an empty dewpond on your right where the path swings slightly away from the fenceline. Now, if you look down to your left you will see the village of Ditchling. At the end of the field, go through the bridlegate and you are now in the Sussex Trust for Nature Conservation Reserve and the track takes you back to the Beacon Car Park approx. $\frac{1}{2}$ mile away.

Acknowledgements:

The maps are based upon the Ordnance Survey Map, Crown Copyright reserved.

Ditchling Westmeston and Streat Footpaths Society would like to thank: Cliff Scott for drawing the maps; Ditchling Village Association for financial assistance; and all those who have 'tried out' the walks and offered their helpful comments!

Quotation on back cover from "Round about a Sussex Village" by Fred. F. Wood (1921).